THE WONDERFUL WORLD OF WORDS

14

Count Quantifier

Dr Lubna Alsagoff

PhD (Stanford)

Marshall Cavendish
Children

Count Quincy Quintillius Quantifier helped the king count his nouns. He helped the king count countable nouns.

I want soldiers!

How many?

One day, the king received a letter from one of the WOW villages.

The people in this village need help.

rice

water

food

Let's send them rice.

Count Quantifier also helped the king count his uncountable nouns.

How much rice?

They must have enough rice for the month.

I shall have the soldiers deliver thirty sacks of rice.

The count and the king together made sure that the villagers had enough food and lots of water.

Quantifiers work with nouns to tell us how many or how much there is.

When you have countable nouns, you can count them using numbers:

one marble

two marbles

seven marbles

Read the clues on the next page. Can you tell how many marbles the children need for their game?

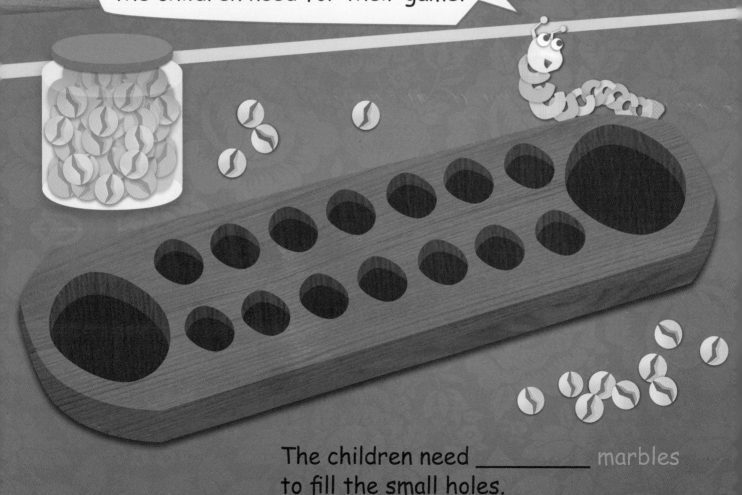

The children need _____ marbles to fill the small holes.

Do we need to put any marbles in the big holes at the two ends?

No. We only need to fill the small holes with seven marbles each.

Every hole must have seven marbles.

Do we have have enough marbles to fill fourteen holes?

There are still so many marbles in the jar.

I think some holes need more marbles!

The carpenter needed to know how many nails to use.

The tailor used quantifiers to count what he needed to sew.

Everyone needs quantifiers.

This recipe calls for two cups of flour and four tablespoons of sugar.

My hens laid thirteen eggs this morning.

The baker needed to measure the flour and sugar to use in her cakes.

The farmer used quantifiers to count things on his farm.

There are many other ways that we can talk about how many or how much.

We can talk about groups of people, animals or things.

band | bouquet | bunch | crew
gaggle | flock | herd | pack

A _____ of zebras   A _____ of musicians

A _____ of geese

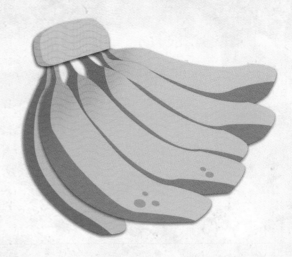

A _____ of bananas

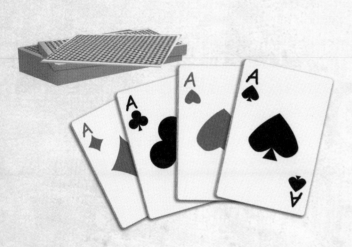

A _____ of cards

A _____ of flowers

A _____ of sailors

A _____ of birds

The soldiers each carried two pails of water.

12

13

Let's try this crossword puzzle on quantifiers.

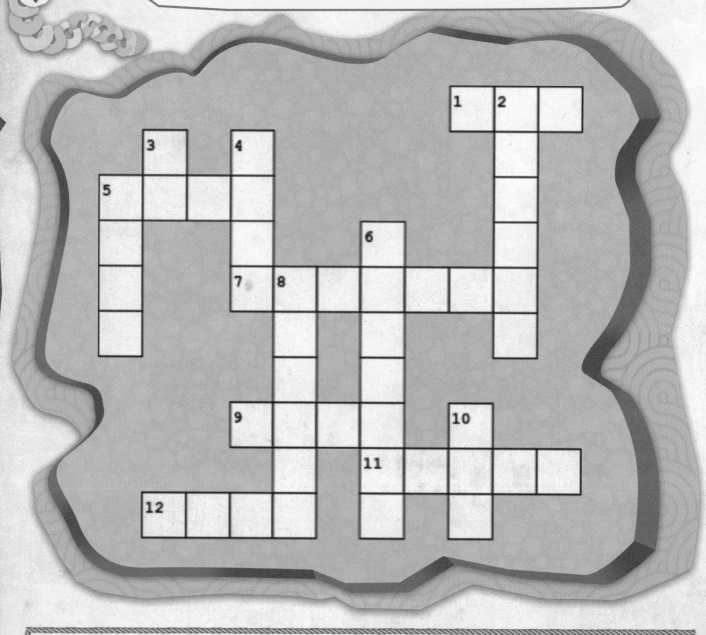

Across

1 Every person or thing

5 A larger number or amount

7 More than a few, but less than many

9 Used with "how" to ask about quantity

11 All the members of a group of three or more

12 Two people or things together

Down

2 A small amount

3 Not any

4 A smaller number or amount

5 A large number of things or people

6 Usually used with "nor"

8 As much or as many as needed

10 A small number of things or people

Look at this picture and use quantifiers to help describe it.

Two | many | three | some | four

There are _____ birds sitting on the turret.

The queen can see _____ hills in the horizon.

_____ horses are grazing in the meadow.

The _____ houses near the meadow belong to the WOW gardeners.

The queen was happy to see so _____ tall, majestic trees along the river.

The Fabulous Forest of WOW

Owl, Donkey and Squirrel were busy at the clinic.

Owl was happy. The animals were all getting better.

We don't need a clinic anymore.

Let's open a school!

The animals came to help.

SCHOOL

They now needed furniture for the classroom.

The animals were so excited. They brought in all the furniture they could find!

Oh dear! There is too much furniture in the classroom.

How many desks do we need?

Let's put twelve desks.

...and twelve chairs.

And don't forget to have one nice large table for the teacher!

The new classroom looked splendid!

We use quantifiers in questions:

How many _____ ?
countable noun

How many eggs are there in a carton?

How much _____ ?
uncountable noun

How much sugar do you need to make this cake?

Try asking your own questions:

How much _____ ?

How much _____ ?

How many _____ ?

How many _____ ?

21

To celebrate the opening of the school in the Forest of WOW, Rabbit decided to bake a cake.

He chose a very simple recipe with only four steps!

Can you find the quantifiers? Underline them in red!

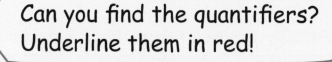

A Simply Delicious Chocolate Cake

Ingredients

2 cups of plain flour
1½ cups of sugar
1 cup of cocoa powder
1½ teaspoons of baking soda
1½ teaspoons of baking powder

2 eggs
1 cup of milk
½ cup of vegetable oil
2 teaspoons of vanilla extract
A pinch of salt

Instructions

1. In a large bowl, stir all the dry ingredients together.
2. Mix in the eggs, milk, oil and vanilla.
3. Pour the mixture into a baking tin and bake in an oven preheated to 180°C for 30–35 minutes.
4. Let the cake cool for a few more minutes before removing from the tin.

All the animals came to celebrate the opening of the new school!

Dear Parents,

In this volume, we learn about quantifiers. These are words that help us count the amount or number of things. With young children, it's best to let them discover patterns on their own rather than learn complicated rules. Ask them about these patterns. For example, notice that in recipes, numbers are written as numerals rather than spelt out.

You can also help your child discover different ways to use quantifiers by learning how to play the game of congkak which I've introduced in this volume. And hopefully, try my recipe for a chocolate cake!

Page	Possible Answers
6	The children need ninety-eight marbles to fill the holes.
10–11	herd | band | gaggle | bunch | pack | bouquet | crew | flock
14	

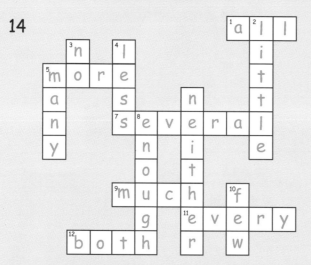

15   four | some | three | two | many

21   Here are some questions I would love to know the answers to!
• How much water is there in a swimming pool?
• How many whiskers does a cat have?
• How many leaves can a caterpillar eat in a day?
• How much sand do you need to build the world's biggest sandcastle?

22   2 cups of plain flour | 1½ cups of sugar | 1 cup of cocoa powder
1½ teaspoons of baking soda | 1½ teaspoons of baking powder |
2 eggs | 1 cup of milk | ½ cup of vegetable oil |
2 teaspoons of vanilla extract | A pinch of salt |
all the dry ingredients | 30–35 minutes | a few more minutes

CERTIFICATE OF ACHIEVEMENT

Volume 14

Awarded to

Name _____

for mastering Volume 14

Date _____

Welcome to the **Wonderful World of Words (WOW)**!

This series of books aims to help children learn English grammar in a fun and meaningful way through stories.

Children will read and discover how the people and animals of WOW learn the importance of grammar, as the adventure unfolds from volume to volume.

What's Inside

Imaginative stories that engage children, and help develop an interest in learning grammar

Adventures that encourage children to learn and understand grammar, and not just memorise rules

Games and activities to reinforce learning and check for understanding

About the Author

Dr Lubna Alsagoff is a language educator who is especially known for her work in improving the teaching of grammar in schools and in teacher education. She was Head of English Language and Literature at the National Institute of Education (NIE), and has published a number of grammar resources used by teachers and students. She has a PhD in Linguistics from Stanford University, USA, and has been teaching and researching English grammar for over 30 years.

Published by Marshall Cavendish Children
An imprint of Marshall Cavendish International

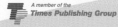
A member of the
Times Publishing Group

Printed in Singapore

visit our website at:
www.marshallcavendish.com

Marshall Cavendish
Children

CHILDREN
ISBN 978-981-5009-03-3

9 789815 009033